The Polar Bear, Chicken Soup and Friends

written by
Doug Brown

© Doug Brown, 2021

First published in 2021
Publisher: Doug Brown

Written by Doug Brown
Illustrated by Gonmuki
Page design by Bryony van der Merwe

ISBN: 978-0-578-98325-7 (paperback)
ISBN: 978-0-578-99395-9 (hardcover)

Dedicated to my beautiful nieces,

Jordyn and Morgan

To my entire family and all my friends, thank you for your encouragement and support. Special thanks to my lovely wife, Karla, for all your patience and input on the completion of this book.

Sincerest thanks to the following individuals for their assistance and support for this book:
Dr. Mary K. Foster, Anne Valente, Elaine Magwood, Mr. Richard Zorn, Joanne Anderson, Sarah Boyce, Bridget Holloman, Tracy Budney, Jennifer Lombardo, Heather Brown, Elizabeth and Harper Tabone, Taylor Flagler, Mr. Trent DeSisso, and Staci Woodley.

On a **large** wintry hill in the **Arctic** lived a polar bear named Bear.

He had **three** friends:

Penguin,

Seal,

and Walrus.

Every day, Bear's friends knocked on his door and asked him to play.

When Bear was ready, they would all walk down to the igloo field to **play ball** near the orca pond.

They always

Walrus would **roll the ball** to Penguin,

Penguin would **roll the ball** to Bear,

and Bear would **roll the ball** to Seal.

One day when Bear awoke, he did not feel well.
He was very tired, he had a runny nose and began to sniffle.

But he **didn't** want to **stay home**, so when
his friends knocked on the door,
Bear was ready.

They **all walked down** to the igloo field to play ball.

Walrus **kicked the ball** to Penguin and

Penguin **kicked the ball** to Bear.

Seal **became upset** and said,
"Hey, you kicked the ball hard on purpose."

"I didn't mean to," said Bear.
"It was an **accident.**
I think I'm catching a cold."

"No! You did it **on purpose,**" said Seal angrily.
"You didn't want me to catch my ball!"

As the two friends **quarrelled**,
the ball **rolled down** the hill.

"**Look, look!**" shouted Penguin.
"The ball is rolling toward the orca pond!"

"**Oh no,** not the orca pond!"
shouted Walrus.

Bear ran as fast as he could after the ball, but he became too tired.
The ball **splashed** into the orca pond.

"My ball, my ball!"

squeaked Seal. "How are we going to get my ball back?
Orca whale doesn't like it when things splash into the pond!"

The friends stood around the pond, **thinking**
of ways to retrieve the ball.

"Maybe we should just get another ball," said Penguin.

"Maybe we should wait until Orca whale is asleep
then swim in and get it," suggested Walrus.

"That's too dangerous," replied Bear. "We might
all get eaten. You know he has big teeth and a great big belly."

"I'll **never** see my ball again," mumbled Seal.

Feeling sad, he went home alone, with his head down.

The next day, while in his home, Bear did not receive **a knock at his door** from his three friends.

Nor the next day, nor the next.

Bear decided to make **an effort** to get the ball back.

As he **walked down** to the orca pond, it began to **snow** and became very **windy.**

When he reached the orca pond, Bear did not see the ball.

He searched and searched but after a while his head began to hurt, his belly ached, and he began to sniffle.

Bear had a cold.

The next day, Bear stayed in bed.

He was **very sad** because he had not seen or heard from his friends.

He began thinking about the
big sneeze
he had while kicking the ball to Seal,
and how Seal did not believe him when he tried to explain.

Suddenly, there was a knock at the door.

Knock, knock!

Bear coughed, "Come in."

The door slowly opened and in peered a small seal.

"Hello," said the seal. "May I come in? My name is Professor Sammy. I am looking for my nephew, Seal. Perhaps you have seen him?"

"No, sorry," replied Bear. "I haven't seen Seal or any of my friends for days."

"Oh my," said Professor Sammy. **"Is everything okay?"**

"I'm feeling **a little down**," said Bear. He told Professor Sammy what happened the day the ball rolled into the pond, and how Seal became upset with him and had walked sadly away.

"I'm sorry to hear that," said Professor Sammy.
"Friends should **not anger** one another. They should be able to
forgive each other and say sorry. A ball or anything small should not
come between good friendships. Friendship is very important.

**Friends need each other,
rely on one another, and
take care of each other."**

Bear nodded and agreed.
He knew Professor Sammy **was right.**

"Perhaps I have something that will make you **feel much better,**" said Professor Sammy.

Bear became curious. **"What is it?"** he asked.

"Throughout my **travels** to different countries, I often receive medicines from good friends. Seals do get the sniffles now and then too, you know. While travelling one winter, I was given a recipe that will work wonders for you. Perhaps you will enjoy Chicken Soup."

"Chicken Soup?" asked Bear.

"Yes, it has been known to cure the common cold. I think you will like the taste."

Bear was **puzzled,** he had never heard of Chicken Soup, let alone tasted it. He did not know what it was. He was used to eating fish.

"No, thank you," said Bear. "I don't think I would like the taste."

Professor Sammy ignored him and began preparing the recipe. First, he heated the pot. Then he mixed in all the ingredients and stirred.

The smell of Chicken Soup **filled the air.**

"Ah, the aroma, isn't it refreshing?"

said Professor Sammy. "I will leave the soup warming. Perhaps if you change your mind, you will have a taste."

Professor Sammy put his coat on, then his hat and his mittens. As he neared the door, he said, "A plum pleasing pleasure, my friend. It was very nice meeting you. I must be off to find my nephew, Seal!"

Bear replied, "Maybe you can look down by the igloo field. He and our friends play there every day."

"Yes indeed, I will be sure to look there. **Toddle-loo, my good friend.**"

After Professor Sammy left, Bear stepped
out of bed and walked over to the pot.

He peeked into it with
great curiosity.
"Looks interesting,"
he thought to himself.

He sniffed.

**"Smells
interesting,"**
he uttered.

He then put his paw into the pot and **bravely** tasted.

"Yum, yum, not bad, not bad at all," he said.

Surprisingly, he liked Chicken Soup.

He poured the soup into a bowl and began to eat.

Shortly after, he began to feel much better.
His headache went away, his belly no longer ached, and stopped sniffling.
He began prancing and dancing around. He sang out loud,

"I like Chicken Soup, I like Chicken Soup!"

He was glad
Professor Sammy
stopped by.
He was feeling
much better.

Later that day, Bear walked down
to the orca pond to retrieve the ball.

The next day there was a knock at the door.
Knock, knock! "Come in," said Bear.

The door opened. It was Professor Sammy again.

"I have a surprise,"
said Professor Sammy.

Bear looked on in amazement as Penguin, Seal and Walrus walked in.
Bear was **so happy** to see them.

Bear looked at Professor Sammy and Professor Sammy looked at Bear.

"Did you?" Bear started.

Professor Sammy said, "Well, yes, indeed I did. Your three friends were at the igloo field talking of how they missed all of you playing together. I explained to them accidents happen and that they should remember that best friends should not stay angry at one another or let small things come between them."

"Yes, indeed," said Bear, "and **I have a surprise.**" Bear walked to the closet and retrieved the ball.

"My ball, my ball!" exclaimed Seal. **"How did you get it?"**

"After Professor Sammy left my igloo the other day, I **walked down to the orca pond.** I saw Orca whale swimming and explained to him what happened the day we were playing. I had sneezed really hard when I kicked the ball, causing it to go over your head. I tried running after it but it rolled into the pond.
It was an accident.

Orca whale said it was okay and if it happens again, please let him know.
He will **gladly flip the ball** back to us."

"That's terrific," said Seal. "Now you and Orca whale are friends."

"Always remember, friends help each other," said Professor Sammy.

Seal then apologized, "I'm sorry for not believing you, Bear."

Bear replied, "I'm sorry for sneezing and kicking the ball hard.
Friendships should last forever."

Bear, Penguin, Seal and Walrus were
all happy and together again.

Bear went over to the pot and poured everyone
a bowl of Chicken Soup.

After a while, the four friends and Professor Sammy all pranced and
danced around each other, singing how much they liked Chicken Soup.

About the author

Doug Brown is a Television Program Director, Independent Film Producer, videographer and video editor. Doug currently works in the Peekskill City School District where he started as a substitute teacher. He also worked as a teaching assistant to elementary age students and has served as a recreation counselor to five and six-year-old children. In 2009 Doug produced a short film entitled, "It Couldn't Be Me", focusing on adolescent health. He enjoys working with children and loves inspiring them to live their dreams. He has a love for children's books and wrote his graduate thesis on the Portrayal of African-American Males in Children's books. Doug Brown holds a B.S. degree in Sociology/Communication and Media from S.U.N.Y. at Old Westbury and a diploma in Video Production from NYU.